Horizontal Architecture

Horizontal Architecture

Alan Faena

Rizzoli
New York

New York · Paris · London · Milan

Reality

Priorities

Patience

Downfalls

Transformation

Surrender

Humility

Expansion

Preface

In this book, you will find an essential formula to create a life aligned with who you truly are so you can expand to your fullest potential.

There is no path without downfalls, no wins without defeats, but if our direction and our priorities are clear, every downfall will be an awakening and every defeat a new beginning.

As the artist of our life, our work is to create a reality and surrender to it with all our being, aware that we have the freedom to live our present to its maximum potential, choosing in every instant who we want to be.

By surrendering, we construct a solid foundation to build the horizontal architecture of our being, transforming ourselves, expressing ourselves with humility, and expanding who we are.

Here I share my own path of discovery, which I will begin again every morning until the end of my days.

Alan Faena, February 2024

Reality is the present

Priorities are the direction

Patience is waiting

Downfalls are awakenings

Transformation is evolution

Surrender is trust

Humility is expression

Expansion is being

1

Reality

For me, life is an immense present moving in silence. Reality is the instant within that movement that accompanies the velocity of being. We are the ones responsible for ensuring that our present reaches its utmost strength.

Being the architects of our reality's creation allows us to own each present moment. Our life is the result of the realities we have constructed for ourselves, and if they are aligned with our being, they will reflect our maximum potential.

A reality is created through freedom of choice. The art of choosing allows us to decide who we are at every instant. Creating a path aligned with our potential is not possible without owning our decisions. It is a daily dance, with successes and mistakes.

It's just as important to create a reality as it is to know how to accept and be responsible for that creation and that present, together with its direction and the weight it carries. If we can't live within the reality we have created for ourselves, we will not be able to sustain it. The key lies in how we build our being so that we can feel at ease with ourselves and live up to our creations. From there, we can begin the conquest of what once seemed unattainable.

To pave our way and construct our architecture of being, every choice must be made from the heart, the gateway to totality. We have to trust that the right answers and decisions are already within us. That trust in our heart leads us to choose the right steps and helps create a framework in which we will feel safer.

Finding that peace with ourselves makes us owners of our creation and gives vision to the movement that allows us to flow. We are responsible for creating the attitude with which we will experience our journey.

Small beginnings are what make the path to greatness sustainable. To expand into this immense present, we need to map our horizontal architecture and discover who we are and what we can rely on in each and every moment.

If we can own our reality and embrace our present in its totality, we will be able to surrender and expand our soul, opening the door to the greatest possible connection with each present, with our being, and with Creation.

Priorities

We are windmills navigating the universe, creating combustion for the movement of Creation. Our intention is defined from the heart. Through our freedom of choice, we are the owners of ourselves, turning intentions into actions.

Priorities direct the action of our intention, helping us to map our path in a straight line and create realities according to our potential. They set the rhythm of our being, so that we can continue advancing based on who we are in each present.

Life is the present in motion. The speed of that movement creates constant friction as we advance through the universe. But when priorities become blurred, the friction reaches a level that overwhelms us and creates a fog in our mind, which leads to dispersion. We suddenly feel as if everything is stopping us and we've fallen behind the rhythm of Creation.

Dispersion increases the level of disconnection we feel because, when we have too many fronts, we lose the straight line of our path. In that zigzag, our life becomes heavier and harder because now the different fronts dictate our velocity instead of us.

Poor choices and misplaced priorities begin to blur our path and distance us from our being. Lost in that back-and-forth, we start creating flawed realities that stand in the way of our journey.

When we feel stuck in that mental fog, we must first stop to identify and let go of what is not serving us before we can set our priorities straight. These priorities, guided by our heart and intention, will get us back on track and into the velocity of the present. Then, none of the realities created will be missed opportunities. And that, in turn, allows us to direct our path and experience each step with greater consciousness.

By defining our priorities with freedom of choice and courage, clarity of mind and serenity of heart will be the drivers of our path.

3

Patience

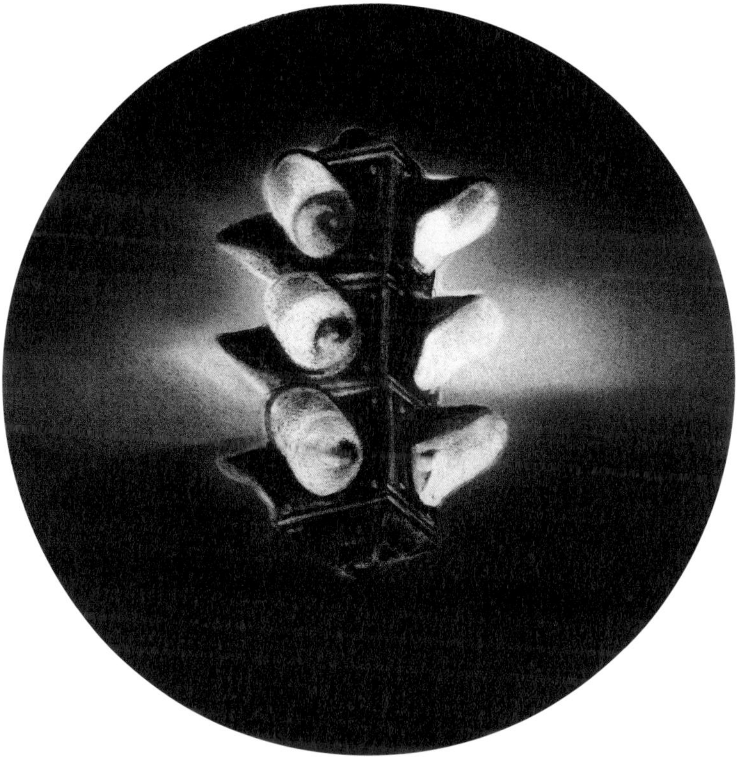

Once a reality is created, patience is the space where our vision clears so that we can make the right decisions.

From the serenity of being and the trust in our freedom of choice, we are able to navigate patience without feeling the need to escape.

There's an art to knowing how to be patient, which happens when we are in solitude. From there, we can create realities that are aligned with our intentions, without interfering distractions.

Our circumstances can make our patience feel longer or shorter, and we can experience it with more or less resilience. Patience is the guardian of our intention. It filters what is from what is not, which is why it requires our utmost attention.

Many times we give up our patience to avoid the anguish brought on by solitude. We speed up our velocity and find ourselves in a sea of distractions. As a result, we lose the focus that each instance of patience requires in order to act with firm intention at the right moment and make the right decisions.

When patience turns into despair, we don't take the time to consider if we are choosing the path to and from our heart. If the intention isn't firm, the ideas become vague, and the heart suffers a lack of courage.

Those who are incapable of patience rush and escape from their center of gravity, fleeing from themselves, clouding their vision, and dulling their understanding. To have patience is to tolerate the void without despair.

To live in peace with patience, we must stop and reconnect with silence.

In learning to be patient, clarity is born.

4

Downfalls

Our center is the heart, the starting point of our vision. When that center falters, life becomes more troubled and confusing, priorities become blurred, and weaknesses take over our path.

As these weaknesses become stronger, they diminish us, make us move away from what we need to face, and taint reality. This stops us in our tracks, leaving us in a hostile place where we no longer own our present and lose our forward direction.

We feel light and eternal when we move at the velocity of Creation; when we slow down or stop, we feel heavy and old, and the rhythm of the universe lets us go.

In that setback, we sense the downfall and lose clarity in our freedom of choice. Poor decisions and the accumulation of mistakes begin to mark our path. Our being becomes discontinuous, we can't make choices, we lose control of our actions, and we get stuck in yesterday's decisions that are no longer valid today. In those downfalls, when we already feel defeated, doubt takes over our mind, leaving us desperate in a meaningless universe, even when the freedom of choice is still ours.

There will always be darkness. It's part of every path.
Yet downfalls are also awakenings. They provide
the combustion to evolve. Life is that friction
between clarity and darkness.

The attitude we take toward our downfalls indicates how much strength we have to find a way out of them. The battle in that instant is to not lose ourselves and to find our way back to our center.

To be is to know how to return. Every life has a moment of peace that we can reconnect with to find our center. We must use it as a new starting point. That will be the light that will help us rebuild ourselves.

Downfalls require patience. By taking the time to find a way back to our being, we reconnect with our priorities and redirect ourselves to keep moving forward. That is the path of the warrior that life demands.

The temple is within us. The prayer is to ourselves. The communion is with ourselves.

5

Transformation

The velocity of the present requires constant transformation to accompany its rhythm and movement. Each day is an opportunity to transform our successes and our mistakes, knowing that every reality created is the result of our evolution, guiding the direction of our lives, and fueling us with its creative energy.

Life's work is moving from one reality to another with the utmost focus to continue owning our choices and being keenly aware of our path. We must maintain ourselves in that state of awareness to construct our next reality with greater wisdom and peace.

Transformation is constant work with oneself,
like a caterpillar that turns into a butterfly. We are past,
present, and future in motion: the time in which
our transformation is reflected. We must accept
who we were yesterday, while being ready to spread
our wings and fly to our next present.

Constant transformation is uncomfortable and oftentimes painful. But that pain mustn't detain us. Everything we let go of in that evolution makes us lighter, amplifies our path, and helps us to modify the motionless past to get back on track with our rhythm and create our next reality.

The goal is to have the capacity to choose freely at every instant what is right for us. This keeps us aligned with our body and spirit so that, with the utmost awareness, we can continue our transformation and become our best self.

6

Surrender

To surrender to oneself is to trust. From there, we make the decisions that will guide us on our path. Therefore, the greatest form of surrender is to have faith in ourselves, which gives us the serenity to live.

We're free to the extent that we surrender our hearts to creating a vibrant reality that allows us to maintain the rhythm of Creation. That trust in our choices upholds the truth of our decisions and the light on our path.

If trust keeps our light, our attitude will be the key to being ourselves when freedom is threatened by external ideas trying to make us waver.

Many times we feel as if the world is telling us to stop through what comes to us as external voices, because we're strangers in an outside that rejects what it doesn't know. If we don't surrender to trusting in ourselves, what reaches us from the outside shakes us like the wind flickering a candle's flame, until it extinguishes us.

Those who stop for these voices are misguided
because life's work is from the inside out.
To battle the external voices that overwhelm us,
we need to surrender to our heart with trust.

There, our decisions will become firmer,
even though they will be unknown to others.
By accepting ourselves as unique, the external
will strengthen us and sustain us on our path.

If there's a place to trust, it's within ourselves. There lie the answers that will lead us to express our sole truth and have the freedom of being to build ourselves, transform ourselves, and evolve. To surrender to oneself is to trust one's own being.

7

Humility

Humility is the expression of our being in motion, that goes from the heart to our priorities. That confidence in the truth that flows from within us allows us to be calm in our present.

Humility is born from surrendering to ourselves—trust is the state and calmness the space that allow us to express ourselves from a place of truth—without needing our actions to be accepted by the outside world. This brings us security in our path and makes us sure of our priorities.

When we walk through life outside of ourselves, our efforts are centered on being liked rather than simply being. We focus on what the external world demands and make decisions hoping for acceptance, which even if we receive it, doesn't fulfill us because it isn't born from our truth.

When we stray from the true work of creating our reality, our growth stops, leaving us frustrated because we don't know where we're going wrong. Losing sight of who we are, we become blinded, drift away from the truth, and start making wrong decisions.

There lies the difference between enlightenment
—the path that comes from the heart—
and dazzlement; the path leading from the outside
to an inner void. A desperate search for an identity based
on acceptance from the outside world. An exhausting,
endless effort of wanting to be without being.

Just as we are blinded when dazzled,
being with humility enlightens our path.

8

Expansion

As the artists of our own lives, the work is the series of transformations that take place within us as we build each reality. The intention at every instant is to find the calmness to carry this out and establish the continuity we need to keep constructing our being.

Expansion occurs when we're able to express ourselves with humility, move with the rhythm of Creation, and build the foundation of our architecture of being. Regardless of where we go, what matters is that our actions elevate our being, realizing that to be is to know how to return to the truth of our heart.

Expansion empowers our present. As we create more and more realities, our architecture grows, and the energy we emanate expands. Achieving this evolution is the only reason for being.

The future is in our hands. We mold our realities day by day and create our movement. This gives direction to our intention and allows us to surrender to the present, which transforms into our future.

In horizontal architecture, we find the formula to create and enact our life in this immense present moving in silence.

Original title Arquitectura Horizontal
Translation Grace Faena

Illustrations Gonzalo Fuenmayor

Design Federico Rozo

First published in the United States of America in 2026 by
Rizzoli International Publications, Inc.
49 West 27th Street
New York, NY 10001
www.rizzoliusa.com

Foreword: Alan Faena
Texts: Alan Faena
Translation: Grace Faena
Illustrations: Gonzalo Fuenmayor

Publisher: Charles Miers
Editor: Alexia Casaús Leppo
Graphic Design: Federico Rozo
Production Manager: Rebecca Ambrose
Managing Editor: Lynn Scrabis

ISBN: 978-0-8478-7616-7
Library of Congress Control Number: 2026907299

Printed in Italy
2026 2027 2028 / 10 9 8 7 6 5 4 3 2 1

The authorized representative in the EU for product safety and compliance is Mondadori Libri S.p.A., via Gian Battista Vico 42, Milan, Italy, 20123, www.mondadori.it

Visit us online:
Instagram: @RizzoliBooks
Facebook.com/RizzoliNewYork
Youtube.com/user/RizzoliNY

FSC
www.fsc.org
MIX
Paper | Supporting responsible forestry
FSC® C013123